I am grateful to God for everything! And I believe that the meaning of life is to make sense of other lives. C.A., you are the meaning of my life.
Lov U

Flavio Laviola
2024

This Book Belongs to:

Test Color Page

www.ingramcontent.com/pod-product-compliance
Lightning Source LLC
Chambersburg PA
CBHW082337270726
48658CB00017B/2875